Eric Liddell

Ellen Caughey

Illustrated by
Ken Landgraf

BARBOUR
PUBLISHING, INC.
Uhrichsville, Ohio

© 2000 by Barbour Publishing, Inc.

ISBN 1-57748-721-4

Published by Barbour Publishing, Inc., P.O. Box 719, Uhrichsville, Ohio 44683 http://www.barbourbooks.com

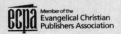 Member of the
Evangelical Christian
Publishers Association

Printed in the United States of America.

Eric Liddell

"THE FLYING SCOTSMAN"

1

The runners were lining up in their positions on the cinder track. Although no lines were drawn to show them where to be, these men had been in enough races to give each other the space they needed.

At least for the moment.

Twenty-one-year-old Eric Liddell of Scotland, known as "The Flying Scotsman," had received a good position just one spot to the right of the most inside "lane." All runners wanted that inside position, especially during the race. Whoever ran there didn't have to run as far, for one thing. And if no one were ahead of you, you would likely win the race.

To win this race meant a lot. The winner today would earn a place on Great Britain's Olympic team and the chance to race in Paris next summer.

Eric glanced to his right and smiled. He knew by name all the runners here, men from England, Scotland, and Ireland, including the man tying his shoes next to him. J. J. Gillies was one of England's best runners, and the favorite to win this 440-yard race. Earlier that day Eric had won the 100- and 220-yard races. No one expected him to win three races on the same day.

As he did with all the runners in every race, Eric offered his hand to J. J. and shook it. But instead of saying "Good luck," Eric said, "Best

J. J. GILLIES WAS ONE OF
ENGLAND'S BEST RUNNERS.

wishes for the race." Eric didn't believe in luck. To him, all things happened for a reason.

Reaching into his coat pocket for a small shovel, Eric then returned to his starting place. Carefully, he carved out of the cinder track two small holes, just the size of the toes of his shoes.

When the race began, Eric would need these holes to help "launch" himself into the race. Most runners brought their own shovels to races. They had practiced carving just the right-sized holes—not too big and not too small—so they could get their best start.

Then, as the runners began to take off their coats and long pants, the race official walked toward the track. Clearing his throat, he proclaimed, "Runners, take your marks!"

Eric felt his heart start to beat faster as he crouched down and placed the toes of his shoes in the holes. He knew that he was a poor starter, and that he would have to run as hard as he

THE RUNNERS BEGAN TO TAKE OFF THEIR COATS.

could to finish in the top three.

But he would never have a start quite like this!

Out of the corner of his eye, Eric could see J. J. Gillies. J. J. was looking at that inside lane, bordered by a wooden railing. As the seconds ticked by, J. J.'s eyes became like slits. *J. J. is determined to win,* Eric thought. *Are my legs strong enough to give him a race?*

With the small starting pistol in hand, the official raised his arm toward the sky. "On the count of three, gentlemen, and then the gun will sound." Seconds seemed like minutes to the racers until the official spoke again. "One, two, three. . ." *bang!*

The runners' arched bodies exploded forward until they straightened, their legs and arms making them go faster and faster.

Fifteen yards into the race, J. J. Gillies made his move, the move he had plotted in his

"ONE, TWO, THREE. . ." *BANG!*

head minutes earlier. But instead of waiting for an opening, J. J. cut right in front of Eric!

In a second, Eric felt himself lose his balance and go flying into the wooden railing—and then roll over two times onto the grass. Eric sat up and shook himself, then blinked his eyes. Across the track someone was calling his name. Then another voice demanded his attention.

"Get up, get up!" yelled two race officials, waving their arms wildly. "You're still in the race!"

Eric couldn't believe it. But he didn't have time to ask why. Scrambling to his feet, he hurdled the railing onto the track. By this time, even the slowest runner was twenty yards ahead of him. *There is no way,* Eric thought, *unless it is God's will.*

And then Eric started running.

First, Eric began swinging his arms so they looked like two very active windmills. Then his

ERIC SAT UP AND SHOOK HIMSELF.

fists started punching the air in front of him, as if the air were holding him back. When his legs really started moving, Eric raised his knees high, as if he were leading a marching band. And finally, to make himself go even faster, Eric threw back his head, his chin up, his eyes looking to the sky.

Yard after yard, Eric began to catch the pack of runners. His arms punching him forward even harder, Eric, to the amazement of the crowd, was now in fourth place. But he was still ten yards behind the leader, J. J. Gillies.

Even though Eric was from Scotland, and was most loudly cheered by Scots, now everyone started cheering and shouting his name. Few spectators could believe what they were seeing.

"Forty yards to go, Liddell!" one man shouted to Eric as he overtook the third place runner. Forty yards, two runners to pass. He

EVERYONE STARTED CHEERING.

couldn't feel his arms or his legs. He could barely take a breath. Forty yards seemed like forty miles to him. But he would not stop.

Again, he willed his hands to punch harder, his knees to lift higher, his arms to swing faster. As he neared the finish line, Eric threw his chest out and his head back one more time— and passed J. J. Gillies to win the race. Eric Liddell had won the 440-yard race by two whole yards.

Eric had used everything he had to win the race. He fell to the ground, gasping for breath, and soon found himself surrounded by the crowd. There were race officials, college friends, reporters and photographers from the local newspapers, and even children.

Eric could only nod or smile at their questions. They were already asking him about the Olympics, about his training program, about his next race. Did he know J. J. Gillies before?

ERIC FOUND HIMSELF SURROUNDED BY THE CROWD.

What would he say to him when he saw him? Everyone could see that Gillies had pushed him off the track.

And then a young voice caught his attention. "Sir, how did you learn to run so fast?"

Eric closed his eyes and a curious expression came over his face. Instead of the endless blue sky, all he saw in his mind were gray stone buildings and matching gray skies. All he could feel was the sadness of the six year old that he had been. A boy who didn't know how to run. A boy very far away from home.

"SIR, HOW DID YOU LEARN TO RUN SO FAST?"

ROBBIE TRIED TO EDGE ERIC CLOSER
TO THE WOODEN DESK.

2

London, England, September 1909

Eric felt his brother nudge him forward ever so slightly. But his shoes felt nailed to the floor, and his eyes seemed stuck on his shoes! Again, but with greater force, Robbie tried to edge Eric closer to the massive wooden desk at the front of the room—the desk of the headmaster, W. B. Hayward.

As Eric raised his blond head slowly and somehow managed to look straight ahead, he spied a pair of kindly old eyes set in a wrinkled face, a face that reminded him of his grandfather. At once, Mr. Hayward arose and offered his hand to both boys.

"Welcome to the School for the Sons of Missionaries, young men! Did you have a good first night here?"

Eric and Robbie looked at each other and then at the floor. Last night was unlike any night they had ever spent—but surely the headmaster knew that.

All new students entering the boarding school had to undergo an "initiation," or a time of testing that the other students had made up. In 1909 at the School for the Sons of Missionaries, the initiation went like this: The older students lined up in two rows, facing each other, with each boy holding a knotted handkerchief. As Eric and Robbie ran between the lines, they were swatted with the handkerchiefs.

Eric and Robbie could hardly wait to get

THEY WERE SWATTED WITH THE HANDKERCHIEFS.

back to the room they shared after that. "It wasn't so bad, was it, Eric?" Robbie had said last night. But Eric hadn't wanted to talk much. "Is it Mother, then?" At age eight, Robbie, a sandy-haired older version of his brother, always wanted to make Eric feel better.

On his metal bed, six-year-old Eric tried to curl up into a smaller and smaller ball.

Eric knew it would only be seconds before Robbie came over to see if he were crying. Sure enough, soon he could hear the padding of his brother's feet crossing the small room. And then he felt his brother's breath against his cheek. "Eric, talk to me. Please."

Slowly, Eric turned to face his brother and his best friend, his dimpled chin quivering. But he said nothing.

"You know, we will have to get used to this. And we will have to pretend when we see Mother that everything is fine."

"WE WILL HAVE TO GET USED TO THIS."

Eric swallowed loudly. "Do Mother and Jenny have to go back to China?"

Robbie nodded. "You know they do. That's where Father is."

Closing his eyes, Eric thought he heard Robbie say good night, even though it had not been a good one at all. He couldn't imagine any night away from his family ever being good.

Headmaster Hayward looked the Liddell brothers up and down, from the tops of their sandy blond heads to the laces on their worn leather shoes. *Robert, or Robbie as he wants to be called, seems so much healthier than poor little Eric,* he thought to himself. *I must do something about this Eric, yes, I must. No six year old should look so pale and so thin! Makes one wonder what life was like in China. . . .*

As if aware of the headmaster's thoughts, Eric and Robbie again gave the floor their most careful attention. But at the sound of the older

HEADMASTER HAYWARD LOOKED
THE LIDDELL BROTHERS UP AND DOWN.

man clearing his throat, both heads shot up.

"I trust this will be a good first term for you both," Mr. Hayward said. "Besides your usual classes, you'll be learning to play rugby, er, rugger, I think the boys call it. Great sport, rugby! Sure to bring out the apples in your cheeks!"

In the month that followed, "rugger" became a favorite sport of both Robbie and Eric, one that they learned quickly. Although rugby is sometimes called "rugby football," the sport is very different from American football. Using an oval-shaped ball—a ball that can be easily bounced and kicked—fifteen-player teams attempt to score a *try* by moving, kicking, or passing the ball down the field and across a certain line. There is no blocking or tackling in rugby and no player on a team may run ahead of the ball down the field.

Sometimes they would have as many as three or four games a week, and many practices

"RUGGER" BECAME A FAVORITE SPORT.

in between. And because there are no time-outs allowed in rugby, Eric was becoming stronger and stronger, a fact observed by the old headmaster.

"You must be liking the breakfast porridge, young man," Mr. Hayward greeted Eric one day as he left the rugby field.

Eric's blue eyes sparkled and he laughed loudly. The headmaster couldn't help but notice that the boy's cheeks looked as if they were painted with pink roses. "Yes, sir," he finally answered.

"Or maybe it's the meat pudding?" the man continued, knowing exactly how most boys felt about that often-served dinner dish.

Eric shook his head wildly, and then ran off as the headmaster shooed him away. *Who would have imagined a few weeks ago,* the headmaster thought, shaking his head. *And it looks as if the boy can run, too!*

MR. HAYWARD GREETED ERIC.

ERIC LIDDELL

During Eric and Robbie's first month at the School for the Sons of Missionaries, their mother, Mary Liddell, had stayed nearby in an apartment just to make sure that her sons were liking school. Now, as the time came for her to return to China to join her husband, she made a final trip to the school.

The occasion was a rugby game, and as most of the boys' parents were serving as missionaries overseas, Mary would be one of the few parents there. Because she didn't want to upset Eric and Robbie, she stayed in the headmaster's office until the game began and then went to the playing field.

She had to see her sons one last time. She had to know they would be all right without her.

There were Eric and Robbie, along with the other rugby forwards, laughing and holding on to each other's shoulders as they tried to kick the ball to the players behind them, signaling

MARY WENT TO THE PLAYING FIELD.

the official start of the game. The boys were concentrating so hard that they never saw their mother. Mary smiled and turned away, pleased.

She didn't want to think about the next time she would see Robbie and Eric. She knew it would be years from now. *God will take care of them,* she told herself. *God will hear my prayers and the prayers of my sons.*

That night as Mary and Jenny boarded a steamer ship for China, Eric cried himself to sleep in his little bed. He had waited until Robbie went to sleep; he did not want Robbie to know.

Someday I'll go back, too, Eric promised himself. *Someday Father and I will work together in China.* And then, finally drifting off to sleep, Eric tried to remember just what China was like.

MARY AND JENNY BOARDED A STEAMER SHIP.

HER FACE MET HIS.

3

Siaochang, China, 1906

"Yellee! Yellee!"

Eric crouched down lower in his hiding spot as he heard the quick, soft footfalls of platform shoes coming closer. He and Robbie loved to play games with their *amah,* and hide-and-seek was one of their favorites. As he heard his Chinese nanny call his name—she could not say "Eric" so she called him "Yellee"—he started to laugh excitedly.

And then her face met his under the table.

"There you are, Yellee," the amah said to Eric in Chinese, tugging at his Chinese-style quilted coat. Laughing herself, she pulled him out and plopped him on her lap. "Enough games for now. It's time for your lessons with Lordie and Jiernie."

Trying not to smile, Eric imagined that "Lordie" and "Jiernie"—Robbie and Jenny—had picked their own hiding places by now. None of them was eager to be in school.

Tagging along obediently, Eric followed his amah to one of the two schools in the mission "compound." One school was for boys and the other was for girls. In China at this time, only boys were given an education. But when the Christian missionaries arrived, they insisted that girls attend school, too.

Surrounded by a high wall made of hardened mud, the compound at Siaochang where Eric and his family lived consisted of four large

CHRISTIAN MISSIONARIES INSISTED THAT
GIRLS ATTEND SCHOOL, TOO.

brick houses, the schools, a hospital, and a chapel for church services. The village of Siaochang, which included the mission compound, consisted of small houses made of mud and another high mud wall, as well as a gate.

The gate remained open during the day. But when night came, the gate was closed and locked. Now there was peace in China—but for years the people of Siaochang had feared for their lives.

Eric, Robbie, and Jenny loved to hear their mother and father tell them stories of what China was like when they first arrived. During the winters at Siaochang, when they spent most of their time indoors, their parents would first read to them from the Bible—and then continue their stories from the night before, stories that usually ended at a very exciting part.

After Reverend James Liddell had arrived in Shanghai, China, in 1898, and Mary Liddell in

THEIR PARENTS WOULD READ TO THEM
FROM THE BIBLE.

1899, they traveled to Mongolia, a northern province of China, to set up a mission station there. Mongolia! The name alone was enough to send shivers up one's spine. It brought to mind jagged, forbidding mountain ranges, never-ending deserts, and wild, roaming peoples.

But there was trouble brewing all over China. A secret group called the Boxers had been organized, a group dedicated to killing all foreigners in China, and especially Christians. The Boxers, who got their name because they made karate-style slashes in the air, believed that Christian foreigners were the reason many Chinese had lost their jobs. Because they believed their bodies could stop bullets and even cannonballs, no foreigner could fight them and win.

At first the Boxers took their message of hate and violence to the countryside, not the big cities. In the country they would tell the

A SECRET GROUP CALLED THE BOXERS
HAD BEEN ORGANIZED.

poor people of China—the peasants—that if they did not do as they said, they would lose their crops because no rain would fall. The peasants were very superstitious and they believed the Boxers.

Six months after James and Mary arrived, the Boxers attacked Mongolia!

In the middle of the night, James and Mary grabbed one small suitcase and rode in a rickety old wagon driven by a mule for many miles. When, after several days, they reached the seacoast, they boarded a boat and sailed once again for Shanghai. But not all Christian missionaries were so fortunate. More than two hundred were killed by the Boxers before the secret group was overthrown.

Shortly after Eric was born and Robbie was two years old, James received his new assignment in Siaochang, a village lying in the Great Plain of northern China, a region known for its

THEY BOARDED A BOAT.

extreme temperatures. Siaochang was one of two mission stations in the Great Plain, an area of more than ten million people (mostly farmers) and ten thousand villages. Eric and Robbie, and later, Jenny, were the only children in Siaochang who weren't Chinese!

At school, the Liddell children were learning the Chinese language, as well as other subjects. Compared to the English alphabet, which has twenty-six letters, the Chinese language, known as *kwan hwa,* has fifty thousand characters or letters. Even to write a simple sentence, Chinese children must learn three thousand characters, or *wen hwa*. For Eric, going to school with his amah meant learning more and more of these strange symbols.

After school, Eric played with his many Chinese friends. He learned how to play Ping-Pong and chess, he learned to use chopsticks to eat, and he learned many Chinese songs. The

THE LIDDELL CHILDREN WERE LEARNING
THE CHINESE LANGUAGE.

people of Siaochang were always singing, whether out in the wheat fields or in their mud houses at night.

Summer 1906 was the last summer Eric would spend in China for a while. The next year James would be returning home to Scotland for what missionaries called a "furlough," or a vacation.

That summer was spent like all the other summers Eric could remember. To escape the intense heat of Siaochang, where temperatures would reach 100 degrees Fahrenheit on most days, the Liddells traveled east to the coast, to the town of Pei-tai-ho on the Gulf of Pei-chili.

Dressed in his one-piece bathing suit held up by shoulder straps, Eric spent his days on the beach, splashing and laughing in the warm water and taking swimming lessons from Mary. In August, James Liddell could join his family because that was the time of year for the harvest

ERIC SPENT HIS DAYS ON THE BEACH.

in Siaochang. People spent time out in the fields and not in church.

News traveled slowly to China in those days, but that didn't bother James Liddell. As he read a prized newspaper from home, he couldn't wait to tell his family the biggest news from Scotland.

"Mary, you simply won't believe this!" James exclaimed, rubbing his graying mustache.

"Father, may I see, too?" Robbie asked, not wanting to be left out. Eric peered over his brother's shoulder, trying to see what had captured his father's attention.

"Wyndham Halswelle! What a name, what a story for Scotland!"

James was greeted by looks of disbelief. "Whozawell?" Eric imitated.

Laughing, James explained. "He's the first Scot to win a medal in track at the Olympics, Eric. You know the Olympics? The international

"HE'S THE FIRST SCOT TO WIN A MEDAL."

sports competition held every four years?" The boys' faces were blank, but James continued anyway. "Well, Halswelle won the silver medal for second place in the 400-meter race."

"Then that means no Scot has ever won first place, right, Father?"

Smiling at Eric's understanding, James nodded. "That's right, son. No Scottish runner has ever won the Olympic gold medal." Thinking a moment, James realized that he didn't want to give Eric the wrong message. He had been happy for this runner because he was from Scotland. But winning a medal at the Olympics wasn't everything.

"Eric, winning a medal isn't *that* important. What matters is *how* you run the race—of life. Do you remember what Paul wrote to the church at Corinth?" Reaching on the sand for his ever-present Bible, James flipped the pages to the New Testament. "Ah, here it is: 'Run in

"AH, HERE IT IS."

such a way to get the prize.' And what prize is that?"

Eric's blue eyes didn't blink. "The prize of heaven, Father."

"THE PRIZE OF HEAVEN, FATHER."

THE SCHOOL FOR THE SONS OF MISSIONARIES MOVED
INTO THE NAVY'S BUILDINGS.

4

London, England, 1912–1920

The School for the Sons of Missionaries was a small school, with no more than 150 students in all. But even so, the boys were outgrowing the gray stone buildings of Eric's earliest memory, and headmaster W. B. Hayward went looking for a bigger "campus."

In 1912, as the Royal Naval School, also in London, moved to a larger complex, the School for the Sons of Missionaries moved into the navy's buildings. Eric and Robbie were excited to find not only more spacious rooms, but more playing fields as well. And there was a track for running, too!

At the same time, the School for the Sons of Missionaries changed its name to Eltham College. (In England, some elementary and high schools are called "colleges.")

Eltham now seemed like home to Eric and Rob, having lived there for more than three years. In those three years, while they had not seen anyone in their family, Mary wrote them often from China. When Rob (and sometimes Eric) wrote back, they didn't have to pretend they were happy for their parents' sake—they were!

Dear Mother and Father—
and Jenny, too,
So far, so good at the "new" school!
Same boys, same teachers (why couldn't

MARY WROTE THEM OFTEN FROM CHINA.

that change?), same schoolwork. You will be pleased when you see my marks for this term (Eric will write you later). Eric is doing all right. Did you know he was in a play? Eric played the dormouse in "Alice in Wonderland" and now everyone is calling him "Mouse"!

But the "Mouse" is not quite like his name. After three years of going through this silly game of knotted handkerchiefs (remember?), your son Eric has finally put a stop to it!

Eric felt sorry for this new boy so he said, "That's enough!" And everyone just stopped doing it. Everyone likes Eric, that's for sure, and I think they think he's different from them (could I tell them stories!).

You may not have heard that Headmaster Hayward has retired.

ERIC PLAYED THE DORMOUSE.

ERIC LIDDELL

(How old was he?) Our new head is named Robertson, and he seems okay except for one of his rules.

This was so funny, and Eric says it's okay to tell you.

It all started when the head said no one could ride his bicycle in the quadrangle.* He said it so many times, we were tired of hearing it. I mean, who would break this rule?

Well, one afternoon when no one was around, guess who comes riding his bicycle in the quad? None other than Headmaster Robertson himself, with his young son on top of the handlebars! I'm sure he thought no one was watching him.

At that moment your son Eric just

---

*The area between school buildings that is like a courtyard, with grass and sidewalks.

**"GUESS WHO COMES
RIDING HIS BICYCLE IN THE QUAD?"**

happened to be gazing out at nature. When he heard the wheels of the bicycle, he couldn't control himself. So he yells, "Hey, no cycling there!" And then he ducks back inside his room.

I hope you're laughing now! Anyway, the head recognized Eric's voice and sent him to his room without dinner that night, but I don't think he's mad at Eric.

We are going swimming again this afternoon and I am excited. As you know, we don't have a pool here at the new Eltham, so we must travel by train to the Baths at Ladywell.* The boys are already after Eric to do his funny routine again. After wrapping a wet towel around himself, he pretends like

---

* "Baths" is another name for a pool.

"WE MUST TRAVEL BY TRAIN."

*he's receiving the "Order of the Bath"
from the King.* We can't stop laughing
because he looks so silly.*

> *Your last letter said we would see
> you soon. We hope so. Eric sends his
> love, too.*
>
> *Your son, Rob*

It wasn't long before the family was all
together again. When Mary, James, and Jenny
arrived in London in 1914—along with a new
baby brother, Ernest—they immediately rented
an apartment for a year. Rob and Eric were only
too happy to move out of Eltham and live with
their family, while still going to school during
the day.

But the year went by quickly and all too
soon the two teenagers found themselves back

---

*An award given to worthy gentlemen for great
achievement.

THE FAMILY WAS ALL TOGETHER AGAIN.

at Eltham as roommates once again. Although they were well liked at school, they were still each other's best friend. And they were still each other's main competition in sports.

Both boys earned their "flannels" and "colours" (varsity letters) in rugby and cricket for each of their last three years at Eltham. In rugby and cricket, they played side by side on a team; in track, however, they were each other's opponents.

Rob was a senior in 1918, and he was determined not to let his little brother beat him during his final year at Eltham. Their closest race was the 100-yard dash. Runners must "sprint" this distance (run as fast as possible) to have a chance of winning.

As usual, the brothers shook hands before the race. Eric wanted to win, but at the same time, he wanted Rob to win, too. When the gun sounded, Rob got off to a better start, but Eric

THE BROTHERS SHOOK HANDS BEFORE THE RACE.

soon caught up with him. The other runners had dropped back. Only the finish line flapped just ahead in the wind.

Throwing his head back and his chest out, Eric crossed the line just ahead of Rob, winning by only a step. He had tied the school record: 10.8 seconds.

Rob, however, was quick to even the score, winning the steeplechase (a combination of hurdles and running), the high jump, and the hurdles. Eric, who later won the 440-yard race and the long jump, was voted Eltham's best overall athlete for 1918.

With Rob at the Medical College of Edinburgh University, Eric became more of a campus leader. At a race in 1919, Eric beat his old record for the 100-yard dash, with a time of 10.2 seconds. That record would not be broken at Eltham for eighty years!

But it was away from the playing fields that

ERIC BEAT HIS OLD RECORD FOR THE 100-YARD DASH.

Headmaster Robertson said of Eric, "He knew what he stood for." Although not required by the school, Eric began attending Bible studies regularly. He also began visiting the sick at a nearby mission. At school, he was a friend to all boys, but especially those who were not as able as he.

In the spring of 1920, Mary, Jenny, and Ernest came home again. This time, they rented a house in Edinburgh, Scotland, where Rob attended the university. Eric had plans himself to join Rob in the fall. That summer, the Olympics games were once again the talk of the Liddell household.

Mary shook her head as her grown sons read every newspaper article, eager for the race times from Antwerp, Belgium. "Who'll be the next Wyndham Halswelle?" she asked, laughing.

Shrugging his shoulders, Rob pointed to

THEY RENTED A HOUSE IN EDINBURGH, SCOTLAND.

Eric, who seemed to hold the papers higher at the mention of his name.

"Yes, Rob, I think he's sitting right here, too," Jenny chimed in.

"I THINK HE'S SITTING RIGHT HERE."

POWDERHALL WAS ALSO HOME TO
GREYHOUND RACING.

5

Edinburgh, Scotland, 1921–1923

Looking around him, Eric couldn't believe a place like Powderhall Stadium even existed. For one thing, the oval-shaped track was paved with cinders, not grass or dirt. Taking a deep breath, he took in the empty stadium stands, the deep blue sky, the perfectly shaped coal-black track, and the yipping sounds of barking dogs! Powderhall was also home to greyhound racing, a popular betting sport in Scotland.

But that wasn't all. Eric almost started

laughing as he watched several athletes prepare to begin their training. As soon as they arrived, they took off their long overcoats to reveal (to Eric) silly-looking baggy shorts. Then they began jumping up and down and stretching their arms and legs in all directions.

As he looked down at his feet to keep from laughing, Eric saw the shadow of a man approaching. And then he felt a tap on his shoulder.

"Excuse me, but you are Eric Liddell, are you not?"

Straightening, Eric looked up slightly to face the older man. "I am."

"Tom McKerchar," the smiling man said, extending his hand. "I'm an athletics trainer at the university. I was told I'd find you here."

As he shook his sturdy, well-muscled hand, Eric was at a loss for words. He had come to Powderhall just to check out the place, not to enlist the help of a full-time trainer. Yes, he'd

"EXCUSE ME, BUT YOU ARE ERIC LIDDELL,
ARE YOU NOT?"

been told he should start "training," but did that mean he had to have someone watching him all the time? "I'm sorry, Mr. McKerchar, but I didn't realize you were told to work with me. I just run, that's all. I mean, what more can you tell me than to run as fast as I can?"

Rubbing his chin, Tom McKerchar looked at the ground and then into Eric's bright blue eyes. "Well, young man, let's just say I've seen you race. . . ."

Just a few months ago, in May of 1921, Eric had entered the University Annual Sports races, his first competition since his days at Eltham. A friend at the university had heard he could run and had talked him into entering. To the surprise of many, Eric placed second in the first heat of the 100-yard dash—and then went on to win the final in that event with a time of 10.4 seconds. To win, Eric had beaten Innes Stewart, the reigning Scottish champion.

ERIC PLACED SECOND IN THE FIRST HEAT.

At the same event, Eric entered the 220-yard race and lost by two inches to Stewart. Little did Eric know that in his entire running career, he would never lose another race in Scotland!

Tom McKerchar had never seen anyone run like Eric Liddell. To Tom, Eric looked more like a prancing circus pony than a world-class runner.

But Tom McKerchar knew he could work with Eric, and he knew he could help Eric run faster even if he didn't change his unusual "windmill" style. First, though, Eric had to want to work with him. Patting him on the back, Tom said, "Eric, you're an unusual young man. Why don't you think about the training and let me know?"

That night Eric asked his mother what she thought. Sitting with him at the kitchen table, she reached for Eric's strong hand. Eric loved the feel of her hands, hands made strong by

ERIC ASKED HIS MOTHER WHAT SHE THOUGHT.

work and years spent in the harsh Chinese climate. Hands that had always calmed him, and then gently urged him in the right direction. Hands that prayed to God.

"Mother, does God really want me to run?"

Turning his hand several times in her own, the older woman then looked at her grown son. "God has given you a tremendous gift, Eric. Of that I am sure."

"But you know my plans. You know that I have always wanted to work with Father in China. How will my running—and now all this training—help me get there?"

"You won't go to China for a few years, Eric. And how long can you run like this? I believe the answer is the same: a few years. Perhaps this *is* God's plan. To run now, and to give God all the glory for your gift."

Eric's face broke out into a huge grin and he nodded his head repeatedly. "You know, when I

ERIC'S FACE BROKE OUT INTO A HUGE GRIN.

run, I do feel like I'm running for God. Guess tomorrow they can start laughing at *me* at good old Powderhall!"

In Europe at this time all athletic training was done only within the confines of a stadium—never in public! It was considered shocking to exercise outside, especially in shorts. So, Eric and Tom met regularly at Powderhall Stadium to train for Eric's upcoming races.

Tom showed Eric how to leave the starting "holes" sooner, how to bring down his knees a bit, and how to cross the finish line most effectively. Most importantly, Tom told Eric not to stop running right after he finished a race but to go a little farther and gradually cool down his body. He instructed him what to eat before a big race (not a big meal!). Lastly, he always gave Eric a massage after his workouts and races. Tom, a trained masseur, would rub the muscles in Eric's back and legs to prevent them from

HE GAVE ERIC A MASSAGE AFTER HIS WORKOUTS.

becoming stiff and sore.

Race after race, Eric began to see how the months of training had helped him. He hadn't stopped winning—and now all of Scotland was cheering for him.

In 1922, Eric set a Scottish record in the 220-yard race, winning it in 21.8 seconds. At this particular competition, Eric entered the 440-yard race as well, winning it in 52.4 seconds. Considered a sprinter, Eric had never competed in that event. Little did he realize how important that would be in two short years!

In the fall of 1922, Mary and James Liddell, along with Jenny and Ernest, prepared to return to China, this time to the town of Tientsin where Eric had been born. As Eric helped them pack what they would need for the trip, he felt far from his usual self. He knew in his heart that they would not be together again for a long time.

ERIC HELPED THEM PACK.

Jenny sensed this, too, but she wasn't going to let Eric dampen everyone's spirits. Dragging him by the hand to her room, the pony-tailed Jenny announced, "I want you to see what I've had to live with the last two years. Just look under my bed!"

Eric began pulling out box after box filled with his trophies. Little did he realize that Jenny, at the direction of their mother, had saved every token of his many victories. There were gold watches, cake stands, clocks, silver knives and forks, and flower vases, too! Eric rolled over on his back and started laughing and laughing.

"I can't believe you've saved all this—and for what?" he exclaimed, almost out of breath.

"No one will ever need a gold watch in this family, that's why," Jenny answered, also laughing. "But from now on, if you win another race, *you* find a place for all the cake stands!"

JENNY HAD SAVED EVERY TOKEN OF HIS VICTORIES.

In 1922 Rob was still in medical school at Edinburgh University with a year to go before he would graduate. After their parents left, he and Eric became roommates once again, sharing a house with twelve other students. But while Eric concentrated on his running and studies, Rob decided to speak out about his Christian faith.

Traveling with other students, Rob visited many cities in Scotland and talked about Jesus. But something was missing from these student-led "crusades." The students needed to have a speaker whose name was known in Scotland, someone who would attract a bigger audience. Someone that even people who didn't go to church would recognize and want to meet.

David Thomson, who was a member of Rob's group, was the first to mention Eric's name. He knew Eric had never spoken in public like this, but there was always a first time.

ROB DECIDED TO SPEAK OUT ABOUT
HIS CHRISTIAN FAITH.

Hitching a ride on a gasoline truck to Edinburgh, David found the house where Eric and Rob were staying. Rob had told David that he couldn't ask his own brother, so David went to see Eric.

The minute David saw Eric, his throat went dry. Eric's picture had appeared in all the newspapers, and his name was always linked with the Olympics, to be held in a little more than a year in Paris. Stumbling over his words, David explained that Eric would be the guest speaker for an audience of all men in Armadale, Scotland.

"Do you, er, I mean, could you come and just say a few words? About your faith, I mean, and oh, your running, too—"

Eric looked at the floor for a minute then lifted his head and smiled slowly.

"All right. I'll come."

Right before David Thomson had approached him, Eric had received this note from

DAVID HITCHED A RIDE ON A GASOLINE TRUCK.

Jenny in China: "Fear thou not; for I am with thee: be not dismayed; for I am thy God. Isaiah 41:10. Love, Jenny." Jenny's faith had given Eric the courage to say yes.

That night in Armadale—April 6, 1923—Eric found he had a gift from God he never knew he possessed. He wasn't much of a speaker, but still the eighty men there listened to every word. And these were men who weren't used to coming to lectures. Unemployment was high in this working-class town, and many men spent their free time in the local taverns, not in churches.

Speaking slowly and quietly, he made the men feel like he was having a personal conversation with each one of them. "Do you want to know the God I love? He has given me strength when I thought I had nothing left. And He has given me these words when I thought I couldn't speak."

Eric looked around the room from face to

"DO YOU WANT TO KNOW THE GOD I LOVE?"

face. "Accept God tonight, and tomorrow you will feel a love you have never known before."

The next day every newspaper in Scotland carried a report of Eric's speech in Armadale. And a week later Eric was asked to speak before a crowd of six hundred! From then on, Eric spent almost every weekend speaking about his faith, and his weekdays studying and training for upcoming races. He loved sharing how God wanted everyone to come to know Him—and all they had to do was ask Him into their lives and their hearts.

While Eric had never felt better in his whole life, there were people who questioned his commitment to running. How would he compete now against the world's best runners? Was he too busy running for the Lord?

ERIC SPOKE BEFORE A CROWD OF SIX HUNDRED!

"I MAY ACTUALLY SPEAK TO
THE PRESS FOR A CHANGE!"

6

Great Britain, 1923–1924

Tom McKerchar slammed down the newspaper in disgust. *If I read one more article like that,* he thought to himself, *I may actually speak to the press for a change!* Tom had made it his policy not to give interviews. *But,* Tom thought, *these writers don't know anything about Eric Liddell.*

Up until the summer of 1923 Eric had only raced in Scotland, and as the competition had not always been "world class," Eric's times were considered just average. Now, as he prepared for his first race in England, there were those who were doubting Scotland should waste the train fare for him to go. How could such a human windmill win an international race?

Tom scanned the Powderhall track for his star runner and smiled at the sight of his high-pumping legs and gently swaying arms. *Eric looks so happy,* Tom thought, *he must be doing what God wants.*

The race on July 6 and 7, the British Amateur Athletic Association Championships, was considered one of the most important races before the Olympics. Held at London's Stamford Bridge Stadium, the race would feature a long-awaited duel: Eric Liddell, still considered the fastest man in Scotland, against Harold Abrahams, England's best hope at the Paris games.

Harold, a student at Cambridge University, was from a German Jewish family. Living in

HAROLD ABRAHAMS WAS ENGLAND'S BEST HOPE.

England, Harold felt he had been treated differently because he was Jewish. If he could be the fastest man in the world, he thought, maybe then he would be treated like everyone else.

Eric, on the other hand, didn't mind if he were treated differently because of his Christian faith. That just gave him one more opportunity to show God's love—to shake every runner's hand and wish him well, to treat every runner the same, and never to use bad language or tell bad jokes. But Eric still wanted to win. If Harold Abrahams wanted to be the best, he would have to beat Eric Liddell.

The stadium at Stamford Bridge was filled to capacity on Friday, July 6, 1923, as the temperature soared to over 90 degrees Fahrenheit. Men were wiping their foreheads with handkerchiefs, while women fanned themselves with paper fans. All eyes were straining to see the runners on the track.

THE TEMPERATURE SOARED TO OVER 90 DEGREES.

ERIC LIDDELL

Eric, the shorter of the two at five foot, nine inches, approached Harold first and shook hands with the tall, dark-haired sprinter. Then they resumed their positions for the 220-yard race.

Earlier that morning Eric had won his first heat of the 220-yard race in 22.4 seconds. The top three runners in each of the two first heats had advanced to the second heat. Eric knew he would have to get a better start this time. Harold Abrahams was known for his good starts.

As Eric dug his holes in the track, he couldn't help but glance at the other runners. But Harold's eyes were on the track, deep in concentration. Closing his own eyes, Eric prayed silently, thanking God again for giving him this special ability.

One Bible verse always came to him right before a race, one that Eric liked to describe as the "three sevens," or seventh book of the New Testament, seventh chapter, seventh verse: "But

ERIC PRAYED SILENTLY.

every man hath his proper gift of God, one after this manner, and another after that." Smiling, Eric remembered that was exactly what his mother had said!

As the race official came into view, Eric focused all his attention on the track. After carefully placing his toes in the starting holes, he raised his muscular legs and arched his back just the way Tom had taught him. And then he waited for the gun.

At the sound of the starting pistol, Harold Abrahams exploded from the line, leading the pack by two yards. Once again, Eric had gotten off to a poor start and he could feel all eyes on him. Swinging his arms, Eric willed himself forward, closer and closer to Abrahams.

From his seat in the stadium, Tom watched the race almost holding his breath, while a stream of perspiration trickled down his cheek. Suddenly, the red-faced Scottish man next to

HAROLD ABRAHAMS EXPLODED FROM THE LINE.

him began jumping up and down. "Look at him now! Aye, he culdna win if his heid's na back!"

As if he had heard his countryman's cry, Eric finally threw his head back, his eyes on the cloudless sky above. Gasps could be heard as the two men pushed to the finish line, each one seeming to throw his chest out farther to gain the advantage.

At the tape Eric Liddell had edged out Harold Abrahams with a win of 21.6 seconds, a blistering pace!

On Saturday, the rumor circulating through the stadium was that Eric and Harold would meet again in the finals of the 100-yard race. Both men had won their first heat of the race— Eric in 10.0 seconds and Harold in 10.2—and now the second heats were about to begin. While Eric set a new British national record in the 100, running the distance in an incredible 9.8 seconds, Harold did not place in the top

ERIC LIDDELL EDGED OUT HAROLD ABRAHAMS.

three of his heat and could not go to the finals.

By the end of the day, Eric had won the 220-yard and the 100-yard events, and was awarded the Harvey Memorial Cup as the best British athlete of 1923. His final time in the 100-yard race of 9.7 seconds was another new British record, one that would not be broken for thirty-five years! Eric Liddell was now the reigning British champion in two track events, and the press would not let him forget that.

On the train back to Scotland, Tom showed Eric the latest newspaper articles. "In a week I've gone from goat to glory," Eric exclaimed, laughing.

"Or from black sheep to world's fastest human," joked Tom. "They're even calling you the next Wyndham Halswelle!"

"Good old Wyndham," Eric remembered, smiling. "Now that's something my dad would like to see."

ERIC WAS AWARDED THE HARVEY MEMORIAL CUP.

Putting the papers aside, Tom stared out the window for a while. "We won't know for sure about the Olympics until the race at Stoke-on-Trent in a couple weeks." Tom turned to look at Eric, and then playfully punched him in the arm. "But it looks like it's you and me, Wyndham, in Paris next summer."

Eric shook his head, laughing. There was so much to think about now besides Paris. He still wanted to travel around Scotland and share his love of Jesus, and then he couldn't forget his studies at Edinburgh University. He had one year to finish his degree, and one more year after that to train to become a minister. And then. . .China!

Retrieving his Bible from his satchel, Eric opened God's Word to 2 Corinthians, chapter 10, verse 17: "But he that glorieth, let him glory in the Lord." As the countryside passed in a blur, Eric tried to focus his thoughts. What was God trying to tell him?

WHAT WAS GOD TRYING TO TELL HIM?

THE OLYMPIC GAMES WERE HELD
IN ANCIENT GREECE.

7

The Olympics

No other sports competition has driven athletes to train harder than the Olympics. Perhaps one reason is that the Olympics has a tradition like no other sports event, with a history that can be traced back to 776 B.C.—more than seven hundred years before the birth of Jesus.

From that date until A.D. 394, the Olympic games were held at Olympia, Greece. Every four years—known as an "olympiad"—the fastest and strongest men in Greece would compete against each other.

Olympia was important because it was considered the "home" of twelve gods, including Zeus, the "greatest" one of all. The Greek people had created these gods to explain events of nature and everyday occurrences, and why good and bad things happened to people. To make these gods "happy," on the first day of the ancient Olympic games the people believed they had to offer sacrifices to them!

In ancient times the Olympics consisted of one day of footraces (running), followed by a few days of wrestling, javelin and discus throwing, and chariot races. On the final day of the games, the fifth, the closing event was a race between men wearing suits of armor.

Whoever won that race was crowned by the high priest of Zeus with a wreath made from olive branches and leaves. After a poem celebrating his victory was read, the winner was

THE OLYMPICS CONSISTED OF FOOTRACES, WRESTLING, AND
JAVELIN AND DISCUS THROWING.

carried home to his native village on the shoulders of his friends. For the rest of his life he would be treated like an emperor—everything he wanted would be given to him!

For more than a thousand years the Olympic games continued like this until, for some unknown reason, the Roman emperor Theodosius did away with the competition.

But in the late 1800s, a period of history when people were again interested in studying about ancient Greece, a Frenchman named Baron Pierre de Coubertin decided to bring back the Olympic games—as a worldwide sports competition. Since 1896 the Olympics have been held every four years—except during the two world wars—but in different locations. And, since 1912, women have been allowed to compete as well.

In 1924, the eighth Olympic games of "modern" times were to be held in Paris, the home of Baron de Coubertin. The baron was so

THE OLYMPICS HAVE BEEN HELD EVERY FOUR YEARS.

excited to have the games in his city that he created a special motto just for that Olympic year, a motto taken not from Greek but from Latin.

"Citius, Altius, Fortius!" (That is, translated into English, "Faster, Higher, Stronger!")

Athletes from forty-five countries would be in Paris, including four hundred from the United States alone, a record number. Who would be the strongest, who would jump the highest, who would run the fastest?

The 100-meter race was considered the test for the world's fastest human. From the United States Charley Paddock and Jackson Scholz were considered the favorites; from New Zealand, Art Porritt was considered a possible medalist; and from Great Britain, Harold Abrahams and Eric Liddell alone carried the hopes of their small nation.

But that was before January 1924—before the timetable for the Olympic races had been

HE CREATED A SPECIAL MOTTO.

released by Baron de Coubertin, and before Eric was faced with the decision that would mark him for the rest of his life!

ERIC WAS FACED WITH A DECISION.

TOM MCKERCHAR CHECKED THE MAIL.

8

The Path to Paris, 1924

For many days Tom McKerchar had been checking the mail at the athletic director's office at Edinburgh University. *The schedule for the Olympics should have been sent by now,* he thought anxiously.

He had heard that this summer Baron de Coubertin wanted the Olympics to last only two weeks, and not the entire summer, as in some past competitions. He also knew that no races would be scheduled for Monday, July 14, a national holiday in France called Bastille Day.

A soft knock on his office door caused Tom to sit up in his chair. "Mr. McKerchar," the athletic director's secretary said, interrupting his thoughts, "I believe it's here." In her hand she waved the official-looking envelope.

Ripping the envelope open, Tom scanned page after page of the lengthy schedule. *There it is,* he thought excitedly, *the 100-meter race. And the first heats are on. . .*

The pages slipped through his hands and fell, one by one, gracefully to the floor. Tom buried his head in his hands for a moment, and then stood, making his way for the door. "Miss Evans, I'll be out for a while. I need to find Eric if I can."

Dashing back inside the office to retrieve the schedule, he then sped out again just as quickly, catching a glimpse of Miss Evans's surprised face. "And don't tell anyone the

TOM BURIED HIS HEAD IN HIS HANDS.

schedule is in," he advised sternly. "We don't want reporters hounding Eric—at least, not yet!"

Eric was at the home he shared with several other students, trying to get in a few hours of studying before he left again with David Thomson to give another speech. Since Eric had made the British Olympic team, the demand to hear him had only increased. To all of Scotland, he was already a hero, the man with the best chance to bring home a gold medal.

Tom didn't know what to say, but that was never a problem with Eric. With a broad grin on his face, Eric began telling Tom about his travels for the Lord. Tom tried to pay attention, but Eric was soon aware that his mind was elsewhere. "What is it, Tom? If you don't mind, I have to say you don't look well," Eric said with concern in his voice.

Tom cleared his throat. "It's just—Eric—I know what you're going to say—but I wish I

ERIC WAS STUDYING.

could change your mind."

"Out with it! Only God can read minds." Eric motioned Tom on with his hand.

"The Olympic schedules came in the mail today. You know, the baron is trying to fit all the events and heats into just two weeks. So—"

"So—what is it, Tom?"

"The first heats for the 100-meter race are to be held on a *Sunday,* Eric. July 6, to be exact."

Without a moment's hesitation, Eric said, "I'm not running." His eyes did not blink, he did not wring his hands, and he did not pace the floor of his room.

Sighing, Tom turned away from him and glanced out the window.

"Tom, do you really know why I can't run? God's Fourth Commandment to Moses said to remember the Sabbath day,* to keep it holy. If I

---

*The day one worships God, usually Sunday.

"I'M NOT RUNNING."

run in a race that honors me or other men, I am not remembering God's Sabbath. And if I start ignoring one of God's commands, I may as well ignore all of them. But I can't do that because I love God too much."

Tom nodded his head. Eric had never raced on a Sunday and he wouldn't change his beliefs now, even for the Olympics. "I'll contact the British authorities. That's the next step," Tom said. "But Eric, are you ready for what will happen? I mean, the reporters?"

"Jesus never said that to follow Him would be easy," Eric answered simply.

In the weeks that followed, Tom and the British sports authorities tried desperately to change the date of the first heats. The French officials, however, refused to do that. Instead, Eric was entered in the 200- and 400-meter races, events that he had won before but that he clearly did not dominate. Two other relay events

THE FRENCH OFFICIALS REFUSED
TO CHANGE THE DATE.

—races that involve four runners on a team— were not considered because their heats also fell on a Sunday.

In the weeks that followed, the attacks by the British press were nonstop. "A traitor to Scottish sporting, to all that Wyndham Halswelle stood for!" proclaimed one paper. Another journalist reported that Eric was not running so he could get more publicity. Again and again, newspapers asked, "Why couldn't Eric run on Sunday and dedicate the race to the Lord?"

Everyone, it seemed, was bothered about Eric's decision except Eric. Even a British nobleman was quoted as saying, "To play the game is the only thing in life that matters."

Eric Liddell had decided he *would* play the game, but on God's terms. All through the winter and spring Tom and Eric trained harder and harder for the two events he would run. And in the back of his mind, Eric quoted over and over

ATTACKS BY THE BRITISH PRESS WERE NONSTOP.

one favorite verse from the Bible: "Whosoever believeth on him [God] shall not be ashamed" (Romans 10:11).

To him, God meant more, much more, than an Olympic gold medal.

GOD MEANT MORE THAN AN OLYMPIC GOLD MEDAL.

ERIC AND THE TEAM ARRIVED IN PARIS.

9

Paris, France, July 1924

Saturday, 5 July. *Today it all begins,* Eric thought as he gazed at his reflection in the window of a storefront. And he saw not only his reflection, but the images of many members of the British Olympic team, all dressed alike. Eric and the team—decked out in cream-colored shirts and pants, blue blazers, and white straw hats—were awaiting the signal to begin marching down the Champs Elysees, the grand boulevard of Paris, and then on to the Olympic stadium, known in Paris as the Stade Colombes.

Taking his handkerchief from his jacket pocket, he wiped away a stream of perspiration from the side of his face. The temperature in Paris was already in the 90s, with an expected high of 110 degrees!

Eric filed into line next to Douglas Lowe, his roommate in Paris and one of the favorites to win a medal in the 800-meter race. Just ahead of him was Harold Abrahams, voted captain of the British track team. More than many runners, Harold had understood why Eric couldn't run on Sunday. Because he wanted others to respect his Jewish faith, he, in turn, respected Eric for taking such a brave stand.

At the Arc de Triomphe the parade of athletes paused while Britain's Prince of Wales (later King Edward VIII) placed a wreath at the Tomb of the Unknown Soldier, a monument dedicated to those who died in World War I.

BRITAIN'S PRINCE OF WALES PLACED A WREATH AT THE TOMB.

Eric felt his heart skip a beat at the entrance to the Olympic stadium. More than sixty thousand spectators filled the stands, and the sound of their applause was like the roar of many oceans.

Nation after nation marched under the "Marathon Gate" into the stadium, led by the first team, the athletes from South Africa. Each team was preceded by its nation's flag and sometimes a band from that country.

Just before Eric and the British team entered, the Queen's Cameron Highlanders began to play their bagpipes and beat their drums. Dressed in Scottish kilts and wearing bearskin headdresses, the Highlanders held special meaning for Eric. He knew he had disappointed Scotland by refusing to run in the 100-meter race. But he still had two races to run. . . .

Finally, Baron de Coubertin gave a short speech and military bands played the French national anthem, "La Marseillaise." Cannons

THE HIGHLANDERS BEGAN TO PLAY.

were set off as the Olympic flag with its five rings was raised into the breezeless sky. The eighth Olympics had officially begun!

Sunday, 6 July. As Eric made his way to the pulpit of the Scots Kirk, the Scottish Presbyterian church in Paris, Harold Abrahams began digging his holes in the cinder track for the first 100-meter heat. And as Eric arrived back at his hotel in the afternoon, an exhausted Harold was receiving his victory massage from his trainer. Harold had made it through two heats and was ready to run the final on Monday. He would be the only runner from Great Britain in the 100-meter race.

Monday, 7 July. Eric tried to ignore the stares from the crowd as he found his seat in the Olympic stadium. He did not have a race to run today, a fact the newspapers had all reported at

THE OLYMPIC FLAG WAS RAISED.

great length. But he did have a race to watch and a runner to cheer—the tall and muscular Harold Abrahams.

Four Americans were also in the 100-meter final, including the favorite, Charley Paddock, and Jackson Scholz, considered almost his equal. Paddock was the current world record holder, clocking the distance earlier this year in 10.4 seconds. He still held the Olympic record, set at Antwerp in 1920, of 10.8 seconds.

Eric squinted his eyes and cupped his hands over his forehead so he could see better. *Harold looks as determined as ever,* he thought. Eric joined in the cheering until the race official held up his gun.

At the sound of the blast, the runners sprang to life, soaring down one length of the track. With Scholz at his heels, Harold fought for the lead, breaking the finish line first. Harold had set a new Olympic record—10.6 seconds—and

HAROLD HAD SET A NEW OLYMPIC RECORD.

won the gold medal!

Jumping up and down in the stands, Eric was happier than most of the excited fans there. In his heart, he knew this had been God's plan. He was to give God glory in his way, as a Christian. And Harold was to show his God-given talent in another. (Harold Abrahams was the first British runner to win a gold medal at the Olympics; no European runner would win this event again until the 1980 Olympics.)

Tuesday, 8 July. Tom McKerchar and Eric shared a taxi to the Olympic Stadium, but their ride was a silent one. *Today is the day,* Tom thought, *for Eric to prove all those reporters wrong, and all those so-called nobles*. His face catching the breeze from the open window, Eric thought, *Today is the day for me just to run my race.*

As they walked around the track, Tom shook

TOM AND ERIC SHARED A TAXI.

his head. "It doesn't look good, Eric. They've just laid new cinders and the track is not packed very tightly. Times should be slower."

"Not to mention the heat! Now I know why my ancestors settled in Scotland," Eric answered lightly. "And please don't look so serious, Tom. This is why I run—to be in races like this."

Shaking his head, Tom found his seat in the stands as Eric joined the other runners for the first heats of the 200-meter race. Later, both men were proved right. The times for all the top runners were slower, but all the top runners came through. The stage was set for Wednesday's 200-meter semifinal and final races.

Wednesday, 9 July. As temperatures again soared into the 100s, Eric again found his place on the track for his semifinal race. In the 200-meter race, runners would make one turn, covering exactly half of the oval track.

ERIC FOUND HIS PLACE ON THE TRACK.

Eric knew this race might be as tough as the final, if he made it there. To his left was the great American runner, Charley Paddock. Paddock had finished in fifth place in the 100-meter race and it was clear he wanted revenge. Harold had run in the first semifinal of the day and barely made it to the finals with a third-place finish. Eric acknowledged his friend on the sidelines with a wave. He knew he couldn't let Harold alone carry the British team into the finals.

At the start of the gun, Paddock leaped ahead of Eric, until Eric put his arms in motion. Then, for a few strides, the men ran side by side. At the finish tape, Paddock edged out Eric, winning the semifinal in 21.8 seconds, just one-tenth of a second faster than the Scottish runner. Eric had made it to the finals—but could he run this hard again?

The finals for the 200 meters were to be held in the late afternoon, but the lane assignments

PADDOCK EDGED OUT ERIC.

were posted soon after the semifinals. Harold would be in lane two, the second from the most inside lane; Jackson Scholz was in lane four; Eric had been given lane five; and Charley Paddock was in the most outside lane, lane six. All in all, six runners had made it to the finals.

As the race began, Eric doubted he had the energy to finish in the top three. Charley Paddock got off to a fast start, followed closely by Jackson Scholz. Harold was somewhere behind Eric, the heat having sapped his strength as well. Remembering Tom's advice, Eric pumped his knees higher and threw out his chest. At the finish line, Eric had edged out two runners to gain third place. He had won the bronze medal!

Eric had become the first Scot in Olympic history to win a medal in the 200 meters, and the first Scot to win any medal since the famed Wyndham Halswelle in 1908. Even the newspapers were kind to him, with one reporter writing,

ERIC WAS THE FIRST SCOT TO WIN SINCE 1908.

"As usual, Liddell did not start too well, but made a wonderfully fast finish."

After hugging Tom and Harold at the same time, Eric quickly made his way down the stairs to the dressing rooms, located below the stadium. There would be no victory laps, no flag waving, no fist pumping. That was not Eric's style.

But tomorrow he would be back on the cinder track. Back to prove he could still run the 400-meter race, even though he was far from the favorite.

ERIC MADE HIS WAY DOWN THE STAIRS.

ERIC WAITED, PACING BACK AND FORTH.

10

Paris, France, Friday, 11 July 1924

Outside the Hotel Moderne, Eric waited, pacing back and forth. He was to meet Tom and a few other British runners there so they could arrive at the same time at the stadium. After Thursday's heats, he seemed to feel every muscle of his body. He had run more races in a few days than he had in a month!

Then Eric saw a familiar face. Running up to him was the masseur the British team had hired just for the Olympics. Occasionally, he had helped Tom give Eric a massage. Eric extended his hand and patted the older man on the back. But the masseur said only a few words and handed Eric a small piece of paper that had been folded once. Then he turned just as quickly to go.

"Thanks, I'll read it at the stadium!" Eric called to him, puzzled that the man hadn't wanted to have a conversation. Shrugging his shoulders, Eric put the paper in his pocket. And then it was forgotten as Tom and the others greeted him.

After the semifinal heats had been run that afternoon, six runners had qualified for the final 400-meter race, to be held at six-thirty that evening. The favorites were two Americans, Horatio Fitch and J. C. Taylor; Joseph Imbach of Switzerland and D. M. Johnson of Canada were also contenders. Guy Butler, Britain's silver medalist at Antwerp in this event, was still in the race but

"THANKS, I'LL READ IT AT THE STADIUM!"

he had injured his leg. With his thigh heavily bandaged, he would not be able to crouch down into the traditional starting position.

And then there was Eric. He had been given lane six for a starting position, the dreaded outside position.

As he plopped down in a chair in the dressing room, Eric had never felt so tired. *In just two hours I'll have to run the race of my life,* he thought desperately.

Reaching inside his coat pocket, he happened upon the paper given to him hours before. Unfolding the now-crumpled square, Eric quickly read the message. Then, bowing his head, Eric whispered, "Thank You, God."

Written with care, the message read, "In the old book it says, 'He that honors me I will honor.' Wishing you the best of success always." The "old book" was the Bible; the quotation was from 1 Samuel 2:30, a verse Eric himself

ERIC HAD NEVER FELT SO TIRED.

had always loved. Yes, he had always tried to honor God, even though he was far from perfect. And while others might think that he expected God to help him win the 400-meter race this evening, Eric knew God had blessed him in countless ways already.

As race time approached, Eric laced on his leather running shoes and walked slowly up the stairs to the familiar cinder track. Deafening cheers arose from the crowd at the sight of the runners, especially the Americans Fitch and Taylor. The stars and stripes of the American flag were waving everywhere Eric looked.

Nudging Guy Butler with his elbow, Eric joked, "Has someone forgotten to tell them that two Brits are still in the race?"

Guy tried to smile. "Look at me, Eric. They know I'll never win with this leg, even if I give it all I have. Besides, this is Fitch's event—he'll be trying to beat his own Olympic record." Just

DEAFENING CHEERS AROSE FROM THE CROWD.

that afternoon Fitch had won his semifinal heat with a time of 47.8 seconds.

The time for the runners' warm-ups around the track was ending as the race official in his long white coat approached the cinder oval. But just at that moment, the blaring of horns and the pounding of drums could be heard from outside the Marathon Gate, the formal entrance to the stadium.

The Queen's Cameron Highlanders had arrived—and no official could stop them from marching around the track! Dressed in their full costume—Scottish kilts and bearskin headdresses —they proceeded to play the traditional Scottish "fight" song, "The Campbells Are Coming."

Eric and Guy couldn't believe their ears or their eyes. All around them, Union Jacks began flying, the symbol of their country. Now the British fans were on their feet cheering, even as the last wail of a bagpipe faded into the evening air.

THE BRITISH FANS WERE CHEERING.

In the minutes that followed, Eric once again went from man to man, extending his hand and wishing them well. The Cameron Highlanders had postponed his ritual, one that he had never forgotten. After all these races, the runners had even come to expect this from Eric. To their amazement, he seemed to mean what he said, too.

Clearing his throat, the race official then extended his arm, the pistol pointed to the sky. All the runners were in their starting positions, all except Guy Butler who was almost standing. Eric looked ahead of him, to the first curve of the track. He knew what he had to do.

There was only one way he would win this race. And only God could help him succeed.

In the stands Tom McKerchar held his stopwatch firmly in his hand. As the gun went off, Tom set the timepiece in motion, his eyes fastened on the track. And then his jaw dropped.

Eric was sprinting to the first turn, leading

TOM MCKERCHAR HELD HIS STOPWATCH FIRMLY.

all the runners by more than three meters! Tom blinked his eyes and looked back quickly. And not only that, Guy Butler, bad leg and all, was in second place, his face wrinkled with pain.

Checking his stopwatch halfway through the one-lap race, Tom clocked Eric at 22.2 seconds. At that pace Eric would have won most 200-meter races. No 400-meter runner in his right mind would run that fast—and still have enough left to finish strong. And then Tom saw what he knew would happen: Horatio Fitch had just passed Guy Butler, and his pumping fists were propelling him toward Eric!

Farther back in the pack, Taylor and Imbach, eager to change lanes, had both stumbled briefly. They were now well behind Johnson, Butler, Fitch, and Eric, who was still hanging on to a slim lead.

Now in the final stretch, Tom began pumping his own fists, imitating Eric. There he was,

ERIC WAS STILL HANGING ON TO A SLIM LEAD.

his face to the sky, arms flailing like twin wind-mills, knees pumping almost to his chest, with the finish tape in sight. Sensing Fitch near him, Eric doubled his efforts, widening the gap between them.

Eric Liddell of Scotland was the first to break the finish tape of the 400-meter race at the 1924 Olympic games, running at the world-record pace of 47.6 seconds! He was five meters ahead of Horatio Fitch. Guy Butler had bravely finished third.

Clutching his sides, Eric slowed to a stop. He had nothing left to give. After a few minutes, he slowly turned around and walked up to Horatio Fitch and extended his hand and then to Guy Butler, who had collapsed on the grass.

As the band began playing "God Save the Queen," the national anthem of Great Britain, Tom raced toward Eric, his arms extended. "You couldn't just win, you had to go and set a world

THE BAND BEGAN PLAYING
"GOD SAVE THE QUEEN."

record!" Tom cried out above the crowd's cheers.

Turning to the crowd, Eric waved briefly. At the end of the race, he had not seen the finish tape—but he had seen hundreds of Union Jacks waving wildly. And now he had brought home the gold medal, the first ever won by a Scotsman. He was not proud of himself, but he was proud of his country.

The following day Eric was in his hotel room working on another speech he was to give Sunday at the Scots Kirk. He had left the stadium as quietly as he could shortly after the race so he could begin writing. There was no medal ceremony —in 1924 medals were mailed to the athletes several weeks after the games—and he didn't want to talk to too many reporters.

But now a knock on the door made him put down his pen. "Tom, I had a feeling you might drop by," he said to his longtime friend and trainer.

ERIC WAVED TO THE CROWD.

Tom was holding an armful of newspapers, his smile lighting up his face. "In case you have any doubts, you're an official Scottish hero!"

Teasing him, Eric began to push Tom out the door. "I don't want to know any more, Tom. Wasn't it bad enough when I was the next Wyndham Halswelle?"

"Aye, that it was. But now you're the next Rob Roy and William Wallace* rolled into one! Listen to this," he continued, reading from the London paper. " 'No longer a traitor to his country, Eric Liddell is the greatest quarter miler ever!' And there's even a quote from the Flying Scotsman himself."

Eric groaned loudly. He had hesitated saying anything to the press for fear his words would sound too proud. But he did want to share his faith in some way. That was why he came to Paris in the first place.

---

*Two Scottish heroes.

"YOU'RE AN OFFICIAL SCOTTISH HERO!"

" 'The secret of my success over the 400 meters,' Mr. Liddell explained, 'is that I run the first 200 meters as hard as I can. Then, for the second 200 meters, with God's help, I run harder.' Spoken like a real hero, if I may say so myself," Tom added.

A few days later, after crossing the English Channel from France to England, the British Olympic team boarded a train for London's Victoria Station. Crowds surrounded Eric as he descended the platform, and then joined the parade as he was carried on the shoulders of his fellow Scotsmen to his next train—the one that would take him home to Edinburgh.

At the 1924 Olympics Eric Liddell had indeed been "Citius, Altius, Fortius"—but he had also been much more. Now God was calling him to a greater race, one in which there would be no medals and no applause.

ERIC WAS CARRIED ON THE SHOULDERS
OF HIS FELLOW SCOTSMEN.

ERIC LAY BACK AGAINST THE CUSHIONED SEAT.

11

Tientsin, China, 1925–1935

At last Eric was alone. He had said good-bye to his "family" in Scotland, those thousands of countrymen and women who had followed his running career, and he would soon say hello to his own family in China. As the Trans-Siberian Railway rattled across the barren steppes of Siberia, on its way from Chelyabinsk to Vladivostok, Eric closed his eyes and lay back against the cushioned seat.

For a year he had been treated like the

Olympic champions of ancient times. First, at his graduation from Edinburgh University, he was crowned with a wreath (not of olive branches but oleaster, native to Scotland) and read a poem written just for him. Then he was carried on the shoulders of his fellow students all around town!

When the day came for him to leave his beloved Edinburgh, again hundreds met him at his home to carry the Olympic champion in a beribboned carriage to the train station. As the train was slowly leaving Waverley Station, he leaned out the window, trying to think of something to say. Mobbed by his adoring Scots, Eric decided to sing the hymn "Jesus Shall Reign Where'er the Sun"—and soon everyone was singing with him!

He suddenly laughed out loud, and then quickly brought his hand over his mouth. Most of his fellow Asian passengers wouldn't understand who he was or what had happened to him.

HE WAS CROWNED WITH A WREATH.

Rolling up his sleeves, he decided to read a report on China sent to him by his father. *It's time to dig my holes for a new race,* Eric thought to himself. *The last time I was in China, I was six years old.*

While the Boxers with their karate-style chops were no more, the Chinese people had a new reason to feel afraid. Although a very small nation, Japan was becoming a world power and was beginning to express interest in perhaps conquering its vast neighbor. In Manchuria to the north, the Chinese warlords with their regional armies were beginning to fight Japanese troops. Soon the entire country might be at war with Japan.

Eric's long journey came to an end in Tientsin, China, and what a journey it had been! From England he had taken a steamer ship across the English Channel, and then boarded a train from France to Russia. On the Trans-Siberian Railway,

SOON THE ENTIRE COUNTRY
MIGHT BE AT WAR WITH JAPAN.

the world's longest train system, he had traversed the width of Siberia, and then boarded yet another train that had taken him to northeastern China. James and Mary, and of course Jenny and Ernest, were also in Tientsin, and Rob, now a medical doctor, was in Siaochang at the mission hospital.

Eric had been born in Tientsin, but he had no memories of the dirty, sprawling city. From the city's Devil's Market, thieves, opium dealers, and forgers traded illegal goods. And from grimy narrow alleyways lined with fragile shacks, the city's poor traded almost anything for food.

At the Anglo-Chinese College, however, where he had received an appointment to teach, Eric would have little to do with such desperate people. He would be teaching science, religion, and sports to the sons of Tientsin's middle class and wealthy families. The school's administrators, who were missionaries, believed that by

TIENTSIN WAS A DIRTY, SPRAWLING CITY.

providing a Christian education for the sons of the most successful, the future of China would be better.

And for a time while Eric was there—before war became a fact of life—that was a distinct possibility.

After the first week of classes, Eric collapsed on a chair in the living room of the house he shared with his parents. His mother was preparing dinner and his father was working on a sermon he would give the following Sunday.

"Eric, you shouldn't be so hard on yourself. You've only been back in China a few months," James Liddell advised him.

"You don't know the latest news, Father. Now the school wants me to teach English, my worst subject. Besides, I've forgotten so much Chinese I can barely talk to my students anyway! How can I tell them about Jesus?" Eric sighed loudly.

"HOW CAN I TELL THEM ABOUT JESUS?"

"The language you learned as a boy will return to you, but you must study every chance you get, son. And as for telling the boys about Jesus. . ."

Eric peered closely at the white-haired minister and missionary. "Yes, Father?"

"Remember your God-given talents, your running, your love of sports. They know nothing about you now—"

Smiling again, Eric slapped his leg excitedly. "I see what you mean! But Father, that means —well, you know what they wear!"

All boys at the Anglo-Chinese College wore the school uniform—a floor-length, long-sleeved, dark blue cotton robe—for all school activities, including sports. That made learning any sport, especially those that involved running and kicking a ball, very difficult. After weeks of wondering what he should do, finally Eric took a drastic step. One day he stood before his students—in a

THE SCHOOL UNIFORM WAS A LONG ROBE.

tank top and shorts!

Running up and down the school's tiny grassy field, Eric showed them how easy and fun sports could be. At first the boys laughed, and then they started rolling up their robes. Desperate, Eric pleaded with the school directors to let the boys wear shorts only for learning sports. When the decision was made, Eric became a very popular teacher.

As the boys' skills increased, Eric noticed another obvious need. The school had no real playing fields for games, and in fact, in the entire city of Tientsin, the second-largest city in China, no stadium existed for athletic competition. A few years later, the Min Yuan Sports Field was completed under Eric's supervision. It was a sports arena modeled after London's Stamford Bridge stadium where Eric had run some of his greatest races.

His students were drawn to him because of

THE MIN YUAN SPORTS FIELD WAS COMPLETED.

his sports skills—and Eric used that love to tell them about his best friend, Jesus Christ. As the months and years passed, even the most difficult boys decided to follow Jesus and to be baptized.

In the fall of 1929, because of failing health, James and Mary Liddell decided to leave the mission field and go home to Scotland. They did not want to go, not when their entire family was at last together in the same country, but they had no choice. Eric had said good-bye to them many times over the years but had never felt so alone.

As he faced his mother at the gangplank to the steamer ship, his voice cracked and he quickly wiped away a tear from his cheek. Mary's face was wet with tears, too. "I will miss you more than I can say," he whispered. His voice stopped as he buried his head in her shoulder.

"Eric, look at me. Perhaps now you can meet someone. . . ."

"She would have to be just like you, you

"I WILL MISS YOU MORE THAN I CAN SAY."

know," he said, winking at her, his sense of humor surfacing again. "So don't hold your breath!"

Eric could joke with his mother, but in the months that followed, he missed their home life, even though he was enjoying his new apartment near the school. On Sundays he attended his father's church where he had recently been appointed superintendent of the Sunday school. Before Sunday classes began, the children would gather for singing, led by Eric himself.

Eric arrived at church earlier than usual on this winter morning in late 1929. He wanted to meet with the new organist to go over some songs he wanted to teach the children. Hearing a door close at the end of sanctuary, Eric turned around. A slender young woman, her short black curls bobbing up and down, was walking rapidly toward him.

A YOUNG WOMAN WAS WALKING TOWARD HIM.

"Hello, Eric," she said softly. "You don't remember me, do you?"

Eric couldn't help but smile at her shining face and mischievous dark flashing eyes. There was something familiar about her. "Has it been a few years?" he guessed.

"Oh, very good, yes, it has. And I was a young girl then, so you probably did not notice me."

Eric laughed and rubbed his chin. "I can't imagine how I'd forget a face like yours. But I'd like to know where we met, Miss, er—"

"Florence McKenzie. And it was Pei-tai-ho, the summer of 1925, right after you arrived from Scotland. I was only fourteen, but you still played games with me and my sister, and, of course, all the other children there. We've just returned to Tientsin for another mission assignment, so here I am."

"Well, Miss McKenzie, shall we begin?"

"YOU DON'T REMEMBER ME, DO YOU?"

Nervously Eric pointed to the music, not sure what to say.

Florence's parents, who were missionaries from Canada, had moved into a house not far from the Liddells' former home. And like Eric's parents, they enjoyed a house full of life, with people coming in and out, a house filled with laughter and singing. Eric felt immediately at home there, even though his thoughts about Florence were far from comforting. Only God knew that Eric had fallen in love.

Florence had loved Eric from the time she first met him, but she also had told no one. Her heart beat faster when she caught Eric staring at her, or when he touched her arm to get her attention.

During the summer of 1930, the McKenzies and Eric, along with many other missionary families, vacationed again at Pei-tai-ho. As soon as he returned, Eric sent a telegram to Mary and

ERIC POINTED TO THE MUSIC.

Jenny—with a very particular request.

A few months later, the package Eric had been waiting for arrived. The McKenzies were due to return to Canada in the next few weeks, and Florence had been accepted at nursing school in Toronto. Eric's furlough was also coming up, when he would return to Scotland. There was no time to waste!

As they were walking to Florence's home after church in late fall, Eric reached gently for Florence's hand. "Flossie, I've got something to say, something I've wanted to say for such a long time."

Eric always called her Flossie when he was teasing her, so Florence wrinkled up her nose. "Oh, no, what is it now, Eric? Am I hitting wrong notes every Sunday?"

Laughing, he stopped and gathered both her hands into his and then kissed her.

"No, no, nothing like that. Anyway, I'm

HE KISSED HER.

trying to be serious. Will you marry me?" he whispered.

Florence threw her arms around his neck and held him close. "I thought you'd never ask!" As she opened the package, lovingly wrapped by Mary and Jenny, she cried in delight at the lovely five-stone diamond engagement ring.

"This is just like the ring my father gave my mother," Eric said. "Because you are the only woman I want to share my life with," he added.

Four years later, on March 27, 1934, Eric and Florence were married in Tientsin, and one year later they welcomed their first child. As he gazed into the face of his newborn daughter, Patricia, Eric smiled at his wife and felt his own eyes fill with tears.

Only God knows the future, but I'm determined that we'll never be apart—unlike my family, Eric thought. *But,* he added suddenly, *only God knows the future.*

THEY WELCOMED THEIR FIRST CHILD.

ERIC RODE IN AN OLD RUSTED TRUCK.

12

From Siaochang to Weihsien, 1937–1945

The old rusted truck managed to sink its tires in every pothole along the dusty country road. Bouncing up and down in the passenger seat, Eric felt his legs and arms ache. He longed to get out and stretch his body. He longed to be back in Tientsin.

More than two years ago the London Mission Society had asked if he would consider carrying on his mission work at Siaochang, the home of his boyhood. Many missionaries had left and the need was great.

But there were so many reasons not to go. Because of the nearing Japanese armies, China's Great Plain had become a dangerous place. Florence and his two daughters—baby Heather was one year old—would not be safe there. Then there was the drought. People were starving to death because nothing would grow on their farms—and people were killing each other just for food.

As the mud gates of Siaochang came into view, Eric thought about himself. *I'm not a village pastor, I'm a teacher. Just because I lived here doesn't mean I'll know how to help these people. Why, God, why am I here?*

Before he had left Tientsin Florence had answered that question for him. She had never known Eric as the Olympic champion, but she did know her husband. "Eric, you knew it was wrong to run on Sunday, and you know it's wrong not to go where God has called you. You

PEOPLE WERE STARVING TO DEATH.

have no choice but to go."

Even though almost thirty years had passed, the people of Siaochang still remembered Eric, and they remembered the wonderful work of his parents. "Thank you for coming, Li-Mu-Shi!" they cried as they circled him. Li-Mu-Shi was the name they had given James Liddell, a name that means "Pastor."

"I'm glad you're here, too," a familiar voice exclaimed behind him.

Turning, Eric gave his brother Rob a big hug. He had left his family but he was not alone. To his surprise, his feelings of despair had vanished and his heart was filled with joy. Yes, he was needed here.

Tens of thousands of people lived in the tiny villages on the Great Plain, villages that had been terrorized by bandits, Japanese soldiers, and the drought. So, week after week, Eric and his interpreter Wang Feng Chou—Eric couldn't

VILLAGES HAD BEEN TERRORIZED BY BANDITS.

understand the rural Chinese dialects —visited different places on bicycle.

Before he and Wang entered a village, they would be asked to recognize one or two Chinese characters written on a blackboard. Only those who lived on the Plain would know what they meant.

Eric had little to give the villagers except a message of hope, a message from God's Word. Sometimes the villages had almost been burned to the ground; other times soldiers were already stationed there. In every town, all men under the age of forty-five had been sent to fight in the Chinese army.

Once, as Eric was holding a church service, the sounds of gunfire echoed close by outside. Instead of giving in to his fear, Eric started singing and soon those present joined in, too. At the end of their service, the people raced outside to their homes, suspecting the worst. But the

VILLAGES HAD ALMOST BEEN
BURNED TO THE GROUND.

Japanese soldiers had been shooting at bandits and were not interested in robbing the people or harming their village.

As 1938 came to an end and Rob was due to take his furlough, Eric learned first aid and took on medical duties as well. The mission had come to be known as a rescue station and Eric wouldn't turn away anyone, Japanese or Chinese.

It was because of this attitude that the Siaochang mission was in danger of closing. By 1939 the Japanese flag hung over the entrance to the mission, in an effort to scare people away. Clearly the Japanese wanted missionaries like Eric out of Siaochang because they prevented them from assuming complete control of the area. By February 1940 the mission had closed forever.

Eric returned to Tientsin, glad to be together with his family, but sad about the situation in Siaochang. He knew, however, that he and Florence would not be together long. The war

JAPANESE SOLDIERS HAD BEEN
SHOOTING AT BANDITS.

was spreading, and China was no place for them to be. Booking passage for his family on a ship bound for Canada, he said good-bye to Florence and his two daughters. He hoped he would join them soon, but he still felt his place as a missionary was in China.

Kissing Florence's dark-haired curls, Eric said softly, "Those who love God never meet for the last time." His mother had said that to him once when she left him at Eltham and he had never forgotten it.

In the months that followed, Great Britain and the United States entered into what came to be known as World War II. Japan, faced with the problem of hundreds of Westerners still living in China, decided to create "internment camps" for them. Westerners were Americans and Europeans —some missionaries and businesspeople—who had not found a way out of China.

But to the Japanese, these Westerners were

GREAT BRITAIN AND THE UNITED STATES
ENTERED THE WAR.

"British and American enemies"—and they would be treated as such. Eric Liddell was now a prisoner of the Japanese, but he was still God's missionary.

On March 30, 1943, Eric arrived at the Weihsien internment camp, hundreds of miles west of Tientsin. He had been allowed to bring only three suitcases. High walls and electric fences surrounded the camp and powerful searchlights circled the area continually all through the night. Eric was one of eighteen hundred prisoners, more than half of whom were children.

All prisoners were assigned jobs to do, and Eric took on more than anyone. Known as "Uncle Eric," he was the children's math teacher, coach and teacher of all sports, minister of chapel services, supervisor of a dormitory—and friend to all.

But as the months passed, he was working too hard and not taking care of himself. Supplies

ERIC LIDDELL WAS NOW
A PRISONER OF THE JAPANESE.

were few and many people at the camp began starving to death. Eric, always muscular and fit, now looked shrunken and painfully thin.

Even though there was no equipment in the hospital to make an accurate diagnosis, the doctors and nurses at the camp knew Eric was dying. And Eric knew it, too. Still, he never stopped smiling, he never gave up hope, and he never lost his faith in God.

Shortly before he died on February 21, 1945, Eric scribbled a message to a missionary nurse. On a small scrap of paper he had written the first line of his favorite hymn, "Be still my soul." The Olympic champion whose windmill style was a study in motion, and whose love of God was known around the world, was finally at rest.

"I have fought the good fight. I have finished the race. I have kept the faith."

So wrote Paul to Timothy. So lived Eric Liddell.

"I HAVE FINISHED THE RACE."